OUR LIVING FAMILY HISTORY

OUR LIVING FAMILY HISTORY

FROM GENERATION TO GENERATION

Our Living Family History

Edited by F. Michael Carroll

Copyright© September 1978
Carriage House Publications, Ltd.
28 Bridle Road
Redding, Connecticut 06896
All rights reserved. Printed and bound in the
United States of America. No part of this book may
be reproduced, stored in a retrieval system or
transmitted in any form, or be reproduced by any
means, electronic, mechanical, photocopying, recording or otherwise without the prior written
permission of the publisher.

ISBN 0-89786-004-7   Library of Congress Card No. 78-61410

Our Family Story

Its Past, Present and Future

This Book is Lovingly Dedicated To:

_____

and Recorded By: _____

_____

Date Started: _____

_____

Table of Contents

From Generation to Generation

Genealogy—the tracing of one's ancestors—used to be the special privilege of aristocratic families. Each generation of a wealthy or titled clan employed a historian who kept a careful register of family members past and present. But today we know that nobility does not hold a unique claim on genealogy. Every one of us is the product of a long and fascinating heritage. Moreover, creating and maintaining a family chronicle need not be the task of a professional genealogist. Your ancestry can and should be something you take pride and pleasure in recording.

Why? You have two parents, each of whom had two parents of their own. These four grandparents, in turn, each had a set of parents, too. Within a short span of four generations, therefore, you can count fourteen people from whom you are directly descended. The plot gets thicker and the relations more numerous as you go back in

time. Everyone, in other words, bears the genes of countless other individuals, each one with different physical traits and distinct personalities. What you are is the sum of what they were, so that tracing your ancestors becomes a process of self-revelation. Whether the focus is on you alone or on the entire family, the investigation answers fundamental questions about yourself: Who am I? Why am I the kind of person I am, looking the way I do, living where I live, and believing what I believe?

In another sense, completing this register is a way of bringing the past to life by recording people and events from your personal viewpoint rather than from the impersonal, public vantage of history books. Most of us know who fought and won World War I and World War II.

But if you or an ancestor took part in the combat or lived through the wartime period, then those distant episodes become vital segments of your own story.

Producing a record of the present is as important as recounting the past. Remember that history is not merely a narrative of bygone years, but an ongoing event in which you and your family are living participants. And whatever facts or memories you set down here will provide a point of departure for your descendents' genealogies—in which you will be a historical figure. If you don't preserve what you know, later generations will be deprived of crucial information. The passage of time, after all, depletes the storehouse of available data, since the people with whom you grew up may be no more than vague names in the future.

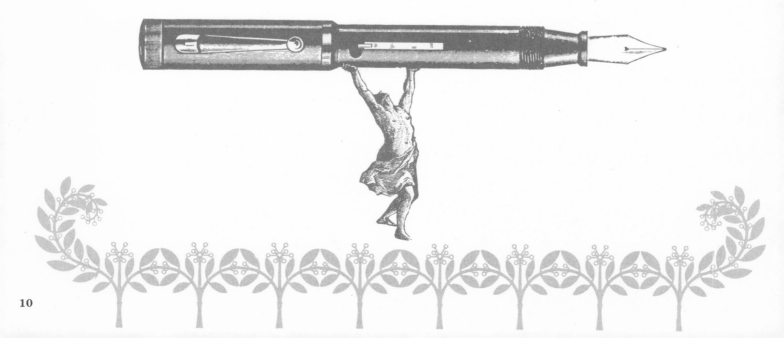

How to Use This Book

The first section is designed to help you make a family tree that fixes your ancestry six generations back to your great-great-great grandparents. Although you may not know all of their names and dates, if you read the chapter on genealogical research at the back of the book, you will discover that with a little effort many of them can actually be traced.

A generation is a step in a person's or a family's lineage that is marked by a birth. When a child reaches adulthood and has children of his or her own, a new generation is created. Family genealogies usually assign numbers to each generation. With respect to your ancestors you may be, for example, the tenth generation in your family line. However, since you are the author of this history, consider yourself the first generation and count backwards, your parents being the second, your grandparents the third, and so on.

Every entry in the genealogical charts is followed by a number that provides a generational code for each particular person in the family. Although it is not essential, you can use these "key numbers" as a shorthand code. Thus, if the husband's father is 3 and you want to identify his brothers, sisters or their children in the section titled "The Family of the Husband's Father," or "Family Gatherings," you enter the key

number 3 followed by the relationship "brother *or* sister—niece *or* nephew" and then the name. This system works for all other sections of the book as well.

In the pages following the family tree you can write a longer, more descriptive account of the people in each generation. This section comprises first the husband's relations and then the wife's. Begin by filling in the vital statistics of the people involved—their names, when and where they were born, and the date and place of their deaths. Because some members of a family, through death or divorce, may have been married more than once, there is also space for the names of the spouses and children of these unions. If your present family is the product of a remarriage, you can thus record those people who form part of your history, but to whom you are not related by blood or in a direct line of descent. Use the remaining space to expand the bare statistics. The ancestors section is followed by twenty-five addtional categories that will enable you to develop a more detailed and comprehensive history. You can limit each category in your own way, describing just yourselves or including other members of the family as well. When you have completed the book, you will have written a unique story, a story unlike any other. This story is the precious record of your heritage.

Our Courtship

When We Met _____

Where We Met _____

Our First Date _____

Our First Gifts _____

The Proposal _____

The Date of Our Engagement _____

Our Marriage

Husband's Name _____

Wife's Name _____

Were Joined in Marriage At _____

Month _____ **Day** _____ **Year** _____

We Were Married by _____

Best Man _____ **Maid of Honor** _____

Husband's Family

Full Name_____

Birth Date_____

Birth Place_____

Full Name of Father_____

Full Name of Mother_____

Brothers and Sisters_____

Wife's Family

Maiden Name _____

Birth Date _____

Birth Place _____

Full Name of Father _____

Full Name of Mother _____

Brothers and Sisters _____

Our Children

_____

_____

_____

_____

_____

_____

_____

Our Grandchildren

_____

_____

_____

_____

_____

_____

Our Foreign-Born Ancestors

Most families can trace their history back to another country. To see your foreign heritage at a glance, list below the ancestors who emigrated from a foreign land. In some cases, your ancestral roots may spread throughout several countries, giving you a rich and diverse heritage. Where did these ancestors come from, when did they arrive, and where did they land? How did the present branch of the family come to settle where it did? And because not all members of a family necessarily emigrate from their homeland, record the names of those who still live in your family's country of origin and how they are related to the people who did emigrate.

The Lands of Our Ancestors

The country or countries where your ancestors came from probably had a different kind of government and different customs from the one in which you now live—and possibly a different language as well. All of these things helped to form the character of your present family, its mode of life, and may even have determined the trade or profession some members took up in the new country. Write down here what you know or have learned about the foreign places where your ancestors were born.

21

Our Family Tree

Husband's Ancestry

HUSBAND'S FATHER'S FULL NAME - 3

HUSBAND'S MOTHER'S FULL NAME - 4

DATE OF MARRIAGE   PLACE OF MARRIAGE

CHILDREN

HUSBAND'S PATERNAL GRANDFATHER'S FULL NAME - 7

HUSBAND'S PATERNAL GRANDMOTHER'S FULL NAME - 8

DATE OF MARRIAGE   PLACE OF MARRIAGE

CHILDREN

HUSBAND'S MATERNAL GRANDFATHER'S FULL NAME - 9

HUSBAND'S MATERNAL GRANDMOTHER'S FULL NAME - 10

DATE OF MARRIAGE   PLACE OF MARRIAGE

CHILDREN

HUSBAND'S FULL NAME - 1

WIFE'S FULL NAME - 2

DATE OF MARRIAGE

PLACE OF MARRIAGE

OUR CHILDREN

WIFE'S FATHER'S FULL NAME - 5

WIFE'S MOTHER'S FULL NAME - 6

DATE OF MARRIAGE   PLACE OF MARRIAGE

CHILDREN

WIFE'S PATERNAL GRANDFATHER'S FULL NAME - 11

WIFE'S PATERNAL GRANDMOTHER'S FULL NAME - 12

DATE OF MARRIAGE   PLACE OF MARRIAGE

CHILDREN

WIFE'S MATERNAL GRANDFATHER'S FULL NAME - 13

WIFE'S MATERNAL GRANDMOTHER'S FULL NAME - 14

DATE OF MARRIAGE   PLACE OF MARRIAGE

CHILDREN

Wife's Ancestry

HUSBAND'S GREAT, GREAT, GREAT GRANDFATHER'S FULL NAME - 63	HUSBAND'S GREAT, GREAT GREAT GRANDMOTHER'S FULL NAME - 64
HUSBAND'S GREAT, GREAT, GREAT GRANDFATHER'S FULL NAME - 65	HUSBAND'S GREAT, GREAT, GREAT GRANDMOTHER'S FULL NAME - 66
HUSBAND'S GREAT, GREAT, GREAT GRANDFATHER'S FULL NAME - 67	HUSBAND'S GREAT, GREAT, GREAT GRANDMOTHER'S FULL NAME - 68
HUSBAND'S GREAT, GREAT, GREAT GRANDFATHER'S FULL NAME - 69	HUSBAND'S GREAT, GREAT, GREAT GRANDMOTHER'S FULL NAME - 70
HUSBAND'S GREAT, GREAT, GREAT GRANDFATHER'S FULL NAME - 71	HUSBAND'S GREAT, GREAT, GREAT GRANDMOTHER'S FULL NAME - 72
HUSBAND'S GREAT, GREAT, GREAT GRANDFATHER'S FULL NAME - 73	HUSBAND'S GREAT, GREAT, GREAT GRANDMOTHER'S FULL NAME - 74
HUSBAND'S GREAT, GREAT, GREAT GRANDFATHER'S FULL NAME - 75	HUSBAND'S GREAT, GREAT, GREAT GRANDMOTHER'S FULL NAME - 76
HUSBAND'S GREAT, GREAT, GREAT GRANDFATHER'S FULL NAME - 77	HUSBAND'S GREAT, GREAT, GREAT GRANDMOTHER'S FULL NAME - 78
HUSBAND'S GREAT, GREAT, GREAT GRANDFATHER'S FULL NAME - 79	HUSBAND'S GREAT, GREAT, GREAT GRANDMOTHER'S FULL NAME - 80
HUSBAND'S GREAT, GREAT, GREAT GRANDFATHER'S FULL NAME - 81	HUSBAND'S GREAT, GREAT, GREAT GRANDMOTHER'S FULL NAME - 82
HUSBAND'S GREAT, GREAT, GREAT GRANDFATHER'S FULL NAME - 83	HUSBAND'S GREAT, GREAT, GREAT GRANDMOTHER'S FULL NAME - 84
HUSBAND'S GREAT, GREAT, GREAT GRANDFATHER'S FULL NAME - 85	HUSBAND'S GREAT, GREAT, GREAT GRANDMOTHER'S FULL NAME - 86
HUSBAND'S GREAT, GREAT, GREAT GRANDFATHER'S FULL NAME - 87	HUSBAND'S GREAT, GREAT, GREAT GRANDMOTHER'S FULL NAME - 88
HUSBAND'S GREAT, GREAT, GREAT GRANDFATHER'S FULL NAME - 89	HUSBAND'S GREAT, GREAT, GREAT GRANDMOTHER'S FULL NAME - 90
HUSBAND'S GREAT, GREAT, GREAT GRANDFATHER'S FULL NAME - 91	HUSBAND'S GREAT, GREAT, GREAT GRANDMOTHER'S FULL NAME - 92
HUSBAND'S GREAT, GREAT, GREAT GRANDFATHER'S FULL NAME - 93	HUSBAND'S GREAT, GREAT, GREAT GRANDMOTHER'S FULL NAME - 94
WIFE'S GREAT, GREAT, GREAT GRANDFATHER'S FULL NAME - 95	WIFE'S GREAT, GREAT, GREAT GRANDMOTHER'S FULL NAME - 96
WIFE'S GREAT, GREAT, GREAT GRANDFATHER'S FULL NAME - 97	WIFE'S GREAT, GREAT, GREAT GRANDMOTHER'S FULL NAME - 98
WIFE'S GREAT, GREAT, GREAT GRANDFATHER'S FULL NAME - 99	WIFE'S GREAT, GREAT, GREAT GRANDMOTHER'S FULL NAME - 100
WIFE'S GREAT, GREAT, GREAT GRANDFATHER'S FULL NAME - 101	WIFE'S GREAT, GREAT, GREAT GRANDMOTHER'S FULL NAME - 102
WIFE'S GREAT, GREAT, GREAT GRANDFATHER'S FULL NAME - 103	WIFE'S GREAT, GREAT, GREAT GRANDMOTHER'S FULL NAME - 104
WIFE'S GREAT, GREAT, GREAT GRANDFATHER'S FULL NAME - 105	WIFE'S GREAT, GREAT, GREAT GRANDMOTHER'S FULL NAME - 106
WIFE'S GREAT, GREAT, GREAT GRANDFATHER'S FULL NAME - 107	WIFE'S GREAT, GREAT, GREAT GRANDMOTHER'S FULL NAME - 108
WIFE'S GREAT, GREAT, GREAT GRANDFATHER'S FULL NAME - 109	WIFE'S GREAT, GREAT, GREAT GRANDMOTHER'S FULL NAME - 110
WIFE'S GREAT, GREAT, GREAT GRANDFATHER'S FULL NAME - 111	WIFE'S GREAT, GREAT, GREAT GRANDMOTHER'S FULL NAME - 112
WIFE'S GREAT, GREAT, GREAT GRANDFATHER'S FULL NAME - 113	WIFE'S GREAT, GREAT, GREAT GRANDMOTHER'S FULL NAME - 114
WIFE'S GREAT, GREAT, GREAT GRANDFATHER'S FULL NAME - 115	WIFE'S GREAT, GREAT, GREAT GRANDMOTHER'S FULL NAME - 116
WIFE'S GREAT, GREAT, GREAT GRANDFATHER'S FULL NAME - 117	WIFE'S GREAT, GREAT, GREAT GRANDMOTHER'S FULL NAME - 118
WIFE'S GREAT, GREAT, GREAT GRANDFATHER'S FULL NAME - 119	WIFE'S GREAT, GREAT, GREAT GRANDMOTHER'S FULL NAME - 120
WIFE'S GREAT, GREAT, GREAT GRANDFATHER'S FULL NAME - 121	WIFE'S GREAT, GREAT, GREAT GRANDMOTHER'S FULL NAME - 122
WIFE'S GREAT, GREAT, GREAT GRANDFATHER'S FULL NAME - 123	WIFE'S GREAT, GREAT, GREAT GRANDMOTHER'S FULL NAME - 124
WIFE'S GREAT, GREAT, GREAT GRANDFATHER'S FULL NAME - 125	WIFE'S GREAT, GREAT, GREAT GRANDMOTHER'S FULL NAME - 126

HUSBAND'S GREAT GRANDFATHER'S FULL NAME - 15

HUSBAND'S GREAT GRANDMOTHER'S FULL NAME - 16

HUSBAND'S GREAT GRANDFATHER'S FULL NAME - 17

HUSBAND'S GREAT GRANDMOTHER'S FULL NAME - 18

HUSBAND'S GREAT GRANDFATHER'S FULL NAME - 19

HUSBAND'S GREAT GRANDMOTHER'S FULL NAME - 20

HUSBAND'S GREAT GRANDFATHER'S FULL NAME - 21

HUSBAND'S GREAT GRANDMOTHER'S FULL NAME - 22

HUSBAND'S GREAT, GREAT GRANDFATHER'S FULL NAME - 31

HUSBAND'S GREAT, GREAT GRANDMOTHER'S FULL NAME - 32

HUSBAND'S GREAT, GREAT GRANDFATHER'S FULL NAME - 33

HUSBAND'S GREAT, GREAT GRANDMOTHER'L FULL NAME - 34

HUSBAND'S GREAT, GREAT GRANDFATHER'S FULL NAME - 35

HUSBAND'S GREAT, GREAT GRANDMOTHER'S FULL NAME - 36

HUSBAND'S GREAT, GREAT GRANDFATHER'S FULL NAME - 37

HUSBAND'S GREAT, GREAT GRANDMOTHER'S FULL NAME - 38

HUSBAND'S GREAT, GREAT GRANDFATHER'S FULL NAME - 39

HUSBAND'S GREAT, GREAT GRANDMOTHER'S FULL NAME - 40

HUSBAND'S GREAT, GREAT GRANDFATHER'S FULL NAME - 41

HUSBAND'S GREAT, GREAT GRANDMOTHER'S FULL NAME - 42

HUSBAND'S GREAT, GREAT GRANDFATHER'S FULL NAME - 43

HUSBAND'S GREAT, GREAT GRANDMOTHER'S FULL NAME - 44

HUSBAND'S GREAT, GREAT GRANDFATHER'S FULL NAME - 45

HUSBAND'S GREAT, GREAT GRANDMOTHER'S FULL NAME - 46

WIFE'S GREAT GRANDFATHER'S FULL NAME - 23

WIFE'S GREAT GRANDMOTHER'S FULL NAME - 24

WIFE'S GREAT GRANDFATHER'S FULL NAME - 25

WIFE'S GREAT GRANDMOTHER'S FULL NAME - 26

WIFE'S GREAT GRANDFATHER'S FULL NAME - 27

WIFE'S GREAT GRANDMOTHER'S FULL NAME - 28

WIFE'S GREAT GRANDFATHER'S FULL NAME - 29

WIFE'S GREAT GRANDMOTHER'S FULL NAME - 30

WIFE'S GREAT, GREAT GRANDFATHER'S FULL NAME - 47

WIFE'S GREAT, GREAT GRANDMOTHER'S FULL NAME - 48

WIFE'S GREAT, GREAT GRANDFATHER'S FULL NAME - 49

WIFE'S GREAT, GREAT GRANDMOTHER'S FULL NAME - 50

WIFE'S GREAT, GREAT GRANDFATHER'S FULL NAME - 51

WIFE'S GREAT, GREAT GRANDMOTHER'S FULL NAME - 52

WIFE'S GREAT, GREAT GRANDFATHER'S FULL NAME - 53

WIFE'S GREAT, GREAT GRANDMOTHER'S FULL NAME - 54

WIFE'S GREAT, GREAT GRANDFATHER'S FULL NAME - 55

WIFE'S GREAT, GREAT GRANDMOTHER'S FULL NAME - 56

WIFE'S GREAT, GREAT GRANDFATHER'S FULL NAME - 57

WIFE'S GREAT, GREAT GRANDMOTHER'S FULL NAME - 58

WIFE'S GREAT, GREAT GRANDFATHER'S FULL NAME - 59

WIFE'S GREAT, GREAT GRANDMOTHER'S FULL NAME - 60

WIFE'S GREAT, GREAT GRANDFATHER'S FULL NAME - 61

WIFE'S GREAT, GREAT GRANDMOTHER'S FULL NAME - 62

Husband's Ancestral Chart

Father's Ancestry

FATHER'S FULL NAME - 3

DATE OF BIRTH   PLACE OF BIRTH

DATE OF MARRIAGE   PLACE OF MARRIAGE

DATE OF DEATH   PLACE OF BURIAL

OCCUPATION

SPECIAL INTERESTS

HUSBAND'S FULL NAME - 1

DATE OF BIRTH   PLACE OF BIRTH

DATE OF DEATH   PLACE OF BURIAL

OCCUPATION

HUSBAND'S BROTHERS AND SISTERS

MOTHER'S FULL NAME - 4

DATE OF BIRTH   PLACE OF BIRTH

DATE OF MARRIAGE

DATE OF DEATH   PLACE OF BURIAL

OCCUPATION

SPECIAL INTERESTS

Mother's Ancestry

GRANDFATHER'S FULL NAME - 7

DATE OF BIRTH   PLACE OF BIRTH

DATE OF MARRIAGE   PLACE OF MARRIAGE

DATE OF DEATH   PLACE OF BURIAL

OCCUPATION

SPECIAL INTERESTS

GRANDMOTHER'S FULL NAME - 8

DATE OF BIRTH   PLACE OF BIRTH

DATE OF MARRIAGE   PLACE OF MARRIAGE

DATE OF DEATH   PLACE OF BURIAL

OCCUPATION

SPECIAL INTERESTS

GRANDFATHER'S FULL NAME - 9

DATE OF BIRTH   PLACE OF BIRTH

DATE OF MARRIAGE   PLACE OF MARRIAGE

DATE OF DEATH   PLACE OF BURIAL

OCCUPATION

SPECIAL INTERESTS

GRANDMOTHER'S FULL NAME - 10

DATE OF BIRTH   PLACE OF BIRTH

DATE OF MARRIAGE   PLACE OF MARRIAGE

DATE OF DEATH   PLACE OF BURIAL

OCCUPATION

SPECIAL INTERESTS

Brothers and sisters play an important role in all our lives because they share our childhood experiences. Any recollections of them, therefore, are part of the individual's own history. So fill in not only the husband's name and dates, but also those of his brothers, sisters, and their spouses. Then try to reconstruct the world in which he lived. Where did he reside? What did he and his brothers and sisters do as children? Did they have any favorite games or hobbies? What schools did they attend? Also record the story of their adult lives—their education, occupations, and places of residence.

The Family of the Husband's Father

_____

_____

_____

_____

_____

_____

_____

Husband's Father's Brothers and Sisters and their Children: _____

_____

_____

_____

_____

_____

_____

_____

_____

_____

_____

_____

Remarriages: Include the dates of divorce or death and the names of Spouses and Children.

_____

_____

_____

_____

The husband's parents most likely had brothers and sisters with whom they were raised. In order to keep a record of this family group, fill in the husband's father's name and dates, those of his brothers and sisters (the husband's aunts and uncles) and their children (the husband's cousins.) On the following page, do the same for the family of the husband's mother. Depending upon the husband's age, his parents were probably born between forty and a hundred years ago. What was the world like when they grew up? What technological advances affected their lives? Complete the picture of the husband's parents with any recollections of memorable personal occasions, such as when and where they met and married.

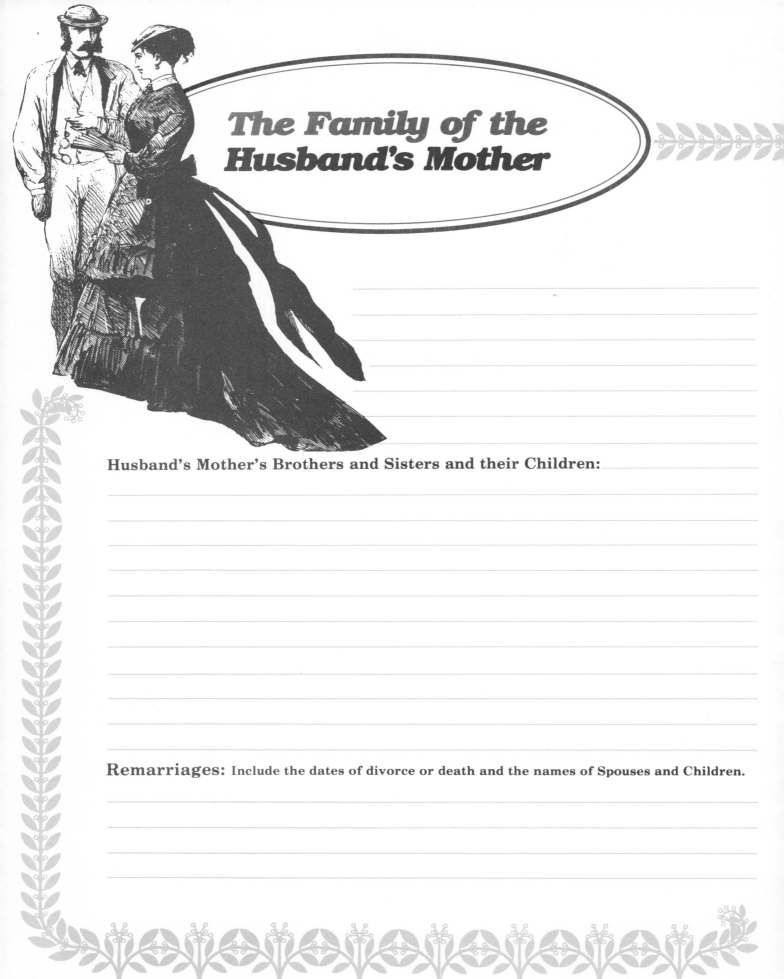

The Family of the Husband's Mother

_____
_____
_____
_____
_____

Husband's Mother's Brothers and Sisters and their Children: _____

_____
_____
_____
_____
_____
_____
_____
_____
_____
_____

Remarriages: Include the dates of divorce or death and the names of Spouses and Children.

_____
_____
_____
_____

The Family of the Husband's Paternal Grandfather

_____
_____
_____

Husband's Paternal Grandfather's Brothers and Sisters and their Children:

_____
_____
_____
_____
_____
_____
_____
_____
_____
_____
_____
_____
_____

Remarriages: Include the dates of divorce or death and the names of Spouses and Children.

_____
_____
_____
_____
_____

The further you go back in time, the more difficult it becomes to find first-hand accounts of one's ancestors. For most people, grandparents are the oldest generation with which they have personal contact. Write in the vital statistics of the husband's paternal grandfather and then of his paternal grandmother. Are there any family anecdotes about the grandparents' early years that tell of characteristic habits, interests, or the kind of lives they led? And in order to keep track of the paternal grandparents' own immediate families, include the names and dates of their brothers and sisters (the husband's great-aunts and great-uncles) and their children. Of course, any personal recollections will make the account all the more vivid.

The Family of the Husband's Paternal Grandmother

_____

_____

_____

_____

_____

Husband's Paternal Grandmother's Brothers and Sisters and their Children:

_____

_____

_____

_____

_____

_____

_____

_____

_____

_____

_____

Remarriages: Include the dates of divorce or death and the names of Spouses and Children.

_____

_____

_____

_____

The Family of the Husband's Maternal Grandfather

_____

_____

_____

_____

_____

Husband's Maternal Grandfather's Brothers and Sisters and their Children:

_____

_____

_____

_____

_____

_____

_____

_____

_____

_____

_____

_____

Remarriages: Include the dates of divorce or death and the names of Spouses and Children.

_____

_____

_____

_____

The husband may also have known his mother's parents—his maternal grandfather and grandmother. Record their names and dates, along with those of their brothers, sisters, and children. Like the paternal grandparents, the maternal grandparents can no doubt remember a childhood vastly different from the husband's youth. They may have lived in another country and have spoken a foreign language. Did the husband's maternal grandmother have the right to vote? Did his maternal grandfather have to pay income tax? Into this historical picture try to incorporate any reminiscences of the maternal grandparents that illuminate their role in the family's life.

The Family of the Husband's Maternal Grandmother

_____

_____

_____

_____

Husband's Maternal Grandmother's Brothers and Sisters and their Children:

_____

_____

_____

_____

_____

_____

_____

_____

_____

_____

_____

_____

_____

Remarriages: Include the dates of divorce or death and the names of Spouses and Children.

_____

_____

_____

_____

_____

_____

_____

_____

_____

_____

_____

_____

_____

The Families of the Husband's Great-Grandparents

_____

_____

_____

_____

_____

_____

Husband's Paternal Great-Grandfather's Brothers and Sisters and their Children:

_____

_____

_____

_____

_____

Husband's Paternal Great-Grandmother's Brothers and Sisters and their Children:

_____

_____

_____

_____

_____

Remarriages: Include the dates of divorce or death and the names of Spouses and Children.

_____

_____

_____

_____

_____

For the husband's great-grandparents, list whatever names and dates are available in family records or can be learned from living parents or grandparents. If grandparents grew up with different customs and witnessed events that are now part of history books, then the great-grandparents lived in an environment even more remote. What was the world like when they were born, a hundred or a hundred and fifty years ago? The great-grandparents probably traveled on horses or in mule carts, or took steam-driven trains and boats. If they had to immigrate to the place in which the family now resides, how long did the journey take? With the help of such projections, the picture of this otherwise distant generation comes into sharper focus.

The Families of the Husband's Great-Grandparents

_____

_____

_____

_____

_____

Husband's Maternal Great-Grandfather's Brothers and Sisters and their Children:

_____

_____

_____

_____

_____

_____

_____

_____

_____

_____

_____

_____

_____

_____

Husband's Maternal Great-Grandmother's Brothers and Sisters and their Children:

_____

_____

_____

_____

_____

Remarriages: Include the dates of divorce or death and the names of Spouses and Children.

The Family of
the Wife

_____
_____
_____
_____

Wife's Brothers and Sisters and their Children: _____
_____
_____
_____
_____
_____
_____
_____
_____
_____
_____
_____
_____
_____
_____
_____
_____

Remarriages: Include the dates of divorce or death and the names of Spouses and Children.
_____
_____
_____
_____
_____

As in the section on the husband's family, the vital statistics of the wife, as well as those of her brothers and sisters, should be recorded here. Were they all born in the same place or did the family move to another town, or even another country? What experiences did they share as children? Recalling a memorable occasion, such as a party or a trip, will help reconstruct the world in which the wife grew up. Did any historical event—a war, an election—affect the family? Finally, note down all the important information about the adult lives of the wife and her brothers and sisters: where they were educated, what hobbies or professions they chose, their residences, when they married, and so forth. Include also the names and dates of the wife's nieces and nephews.

The Family of the Wife's Father

Wife's Father's Brothers and Sisters and their Children:

Remarriages: Include the dates of divorce or death and the names of Spouses and Children.

The world in which the wife's father and mother grew up may have been very different from hers, but at the same time it determined the course of her life. When and where were her parents born? Where did they meet and when did they marry? Parents often remind their children about how things have changed since their own youth. Perhaps the wife's mother or father witnessed the invention of sound movies or the development of commercial aviation. The wife's parents were once part of another family, some of whose members the wife may have known or still knows. In order to complete this picture of the wife's parents' family, fill in the names and dates of her parents' brothers and sisters (her aunts and uncles) and those of their children (her cousins) along with any other interesting information.

The Family of the Wife's Mother

Wife's Mother's Brothers and Sisters and their Children:

rriages: Include the dates of divorce or death and the names of Spouses and Children.

The Family of the Wife's Paternal Grandfather

Wife's Paternal Grandfather's Brothers and Sisters and their Children:

Remarriages: Include the dates of divorce or death and the names of Spouses and Children.

After writing down the vital statistics of the wife's paternal grandfather and grandmother —along with those of any brothers, sisters, and children—try to recollect what is known about the grandparents' early years. Did they live in a large town or a small one, or did they perhaps grow up on a farm? What kind of schools did they attend and what occupations did they train for? If the wife knew or still knows her paternal grandparents, they may have supplied some of this information directly. Such personal accounts help to create a fuller and more accurate picture of the paternal grandparents' generation.

The Family of the Wife's Paternal Grandmother

Wife's Paternal Grandmother's Brothers and Sisters and their Children:

rriages: Include the dates of divorce or death and the names of Spouses and Children.

The Family of the Wife's Maternal Grandfather

Wife's Maternal Grandfather's Brothers and Sisters and their Children:

Remarriages: Include the dates of divorce or death and the names of Spouses and Children.

The wife's mother's parents—her maternal grandparents—were also part of a generation that grew up unaccustomed to many things we take for granted today. Once the names and dates of the maternal grandparents, their brothers, sisters, and children have been filled in, think about the kind of lives they led as youths and how this affected their view of the world. Remember that the wife's maternal grandmother may have been born at a time when women's skirts always reached below the ankles, when bikinis were unheard of, and when landing men on the moon was strictly the stuff of science fiction.

The Family of the Wife's Maternal Grandmother

Wife's Maternal Grandmother's Brothers and Sisters and their Children:

rriages: Include the dates of divorce or death and the names of Spouses and Children.

The Families of the *Wife's* Great-Grandparents

Wife's Paternal Great-Grandfather's Brothers and Sisters and their Children:

Wife's Paternal Great-Grandmother's Brothers and Sisters and their Children:

Remarriages: Include the dates of divorce or death and the names of Spouses and Children.

The wife's great-grandparents, like the husband's, were most likely born in the 19th century, perhaps even as early as 1850. At that time, there were few large cities, the world's population being predominantly agricultural. Did the people whose names and dates appear here own or work on a farm? And how did they communicate with friends and relatives? The telephone, after all, was not perfected until the 1870s and did not become a household feature until after World War I. Do any letters written by the wife's great-grandparents survive? Or are there any stories handed down about their personalities, their accomplishments, or their relationships with other members of the family?

The Families of the Wife's Great-Grandparents

Wife's Maternal Great-Grandfather's Brothers and Sisters and their Children:

Wife's Maternal Grandmother's Brothers and Sisters and their Children:

rriages: Include the dates of divorce or death and the names of Spouses and Children.

Family Weddings

Weddings are joyous events in every family. They not only provide an opportunity for the family to gather together and celebrate, but each wedding also opens a new chapter in the family history. The bride and groom, having left their immediate families, are about to start a family of their own—to add another branch to the genealogical tree. Keeping an account of these occasions is therefore a major contribution to your family's records. So try to expand the list of names and dates with recollections of the wedding party or reception, where the ceremony took place, and the friends and relatives who attended.

Family Weddings

CONTINUED

Other Religious Ceremonies in Our Family

Religious ceremonies usually mark off important milestones in children's lives. Whether baptism or circumcision, communion or bar mitzvah, these events are memorable stations on the road to adulthood. In the space below, fill in the names of the children (including yourselves), the kind of ceremony held, where and when it took place, as well as the names of any godparents or sponsors and a brief description of how the occasion was celebrated.

Our Family's Religious Affiliations

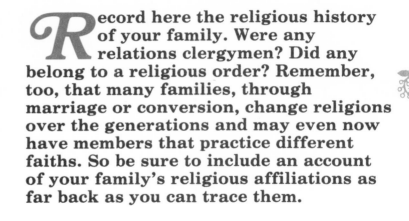

ecord here the religious history of your family. Were any relations clergymen? Did any belong to a religious order? Remember, too, that many families, through marriage or conversion, change religions over the generations and may even now have members that practice different faiths. So be sure to include an account of your family's religious affiliations as far back as you can trace them.

re We Have Worshipped

Use this page to record your family's places of worship—the names of the congregations, their locations, the clergymen, and the period during which you and your family attended. Include also any information that describes your family's role in the church or synagogue. Did you or any other member, for example, participate in the activities or administration of the congregation?

Special Memories

A family history such as this is bound to include references to people who have died, and of whom you have no personal recollections. But at the same time there will be others whom you did know, with whom you shared very special conversations and experiences. In order to preserve this information for yourselves and provide future generations with a living picture of their ancestors, write down the names of these people and your memories of them.

Special Memories

CONTINUED

Our Family's Homes

A record of your family's residences discloses a great deal about its history and activities. So add to the list of addresses and dates any facts that will enrich the account. Why did you or your family move? Was the new house or apartment larger or smaller? Was it in the city or in the country? Did the move affect you or others in a special way—for instance, causing a change in schools or jobs?

Street Address

City   State

Date of Purchase   Resided from   to

Street Address

City   State

Date of Purchase   Resided from   to

Address

State
Purchase   Resided from   to

Address

State
Purchase   Resided from   to

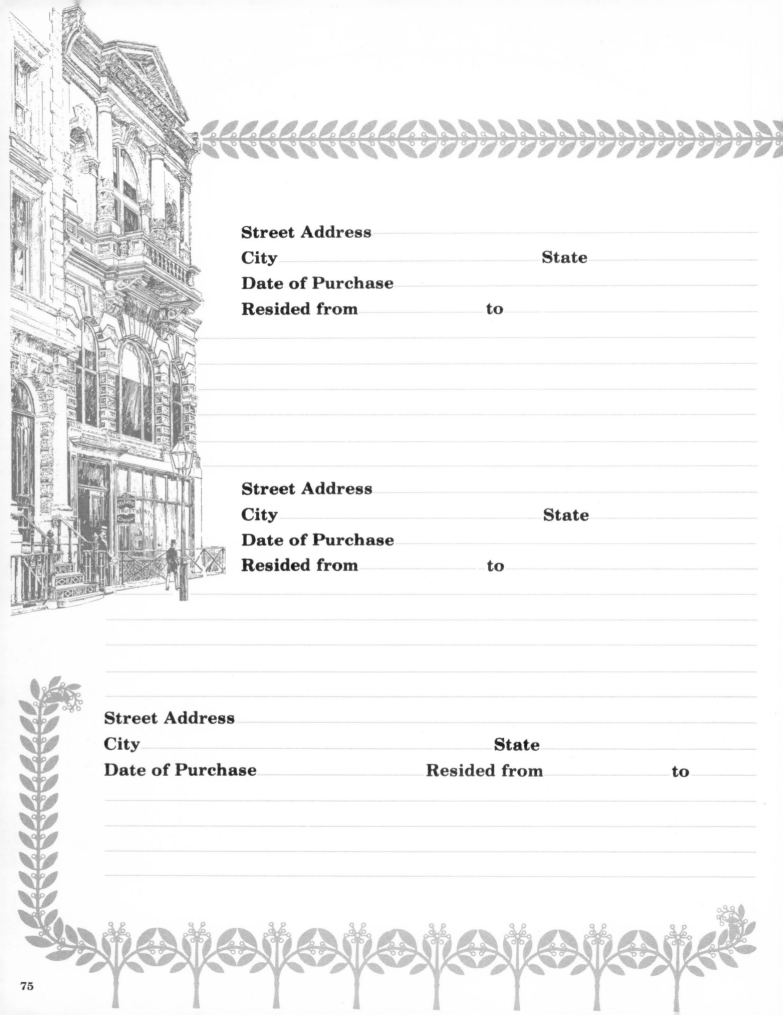

Street Address

City   **State**

Date of Purchase

Resided from   **to**

Street Address

City   **State**

Date of Purchase

Resided from   **to**

Street Address

City   **State**

Date of Purchase   **Resided from**   **to**

Our Family's Homes

CONTINUED

Address

State

f Purchase   Resided from   to

Address

State

f Purchase
d from   to

Address

State

f Purchase
ed from   to

The Schools We Have Attended

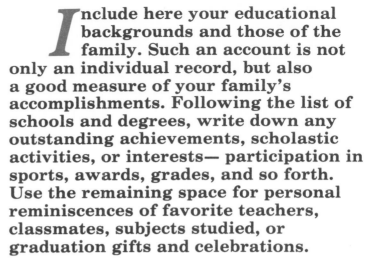

*I*nclude here your educational backgrounds and those of the family. Such an account is not only an individual record, but also a good measure of your family's accomplishments. Following the list of schools and degrees, write down any outstanding achievements, scholastic activities, or interests— participation in sports, awards, grades, and so forth. Use the remaining space for personal reminiscences of favorite teachers, classmates, subjects studied, or graduation gifts and celebrations.

Name	School	Date Graduated	Degree
1			
2			
3			
4			
5			
6			
7			
8			
9			
10			
11			

	Name	School	Date Graduated	Degree
1				
2				
3				
4				
5				
6				
7				
8				
9				
10				
11				

The Schools We Have Attended

CONTINUED

The Organizations We Have Joined

People have always sought out others with whom to share interests or work for a common cause. In the last hundred or so years, as people acquired more and more leisure time, they organized professionally and formed clubs to pursue their hobbies, publicize their political views, or collect charity. By writing down the names of the organizations to which you and other family members belonged, along with recollections of the person or the group, you can retell the story of your family's role in the life of the community.

Professions, Occupations, Crafts & Trades

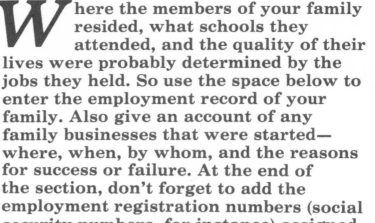

Where the members of your family resided, what schools they attended, and the quality of their lives were probably determined by the jobs they held. So use the space below to enter the employment record of your family. Also give an account of any family businesses that were started—where, when, by whom, and the reasons for success or failure. At the end of the section, don't forget to add the employment registration numbers (social security numbers, for instance) assigned to each person by the government. Many government bureaus file documents according to such numbers, so the list will be invaluable for others.

Professions, Occupations Crafts & Trades

CONTINUED

Our Family's Military Service Record

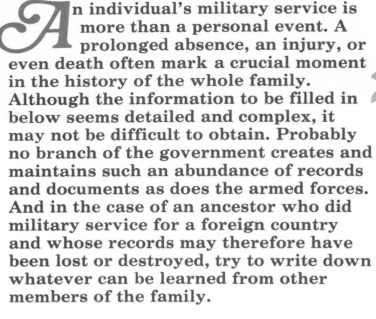

An individual's military service is more than a personal event. A prolonged absence, an injury, or even death often mark a crucial moment in the history of the whole family. Although the information to be filled in below seems detailed and complex, it may not be difficult to obtain. Probably no branch of the government creates and maintains such an abundance of records and documents as does the armed forces. And in the case of an ancestor who did military service for a foreign country and whose records may therefore have been lost or destroyed, try to write down whatever can be learned from other members of the family.

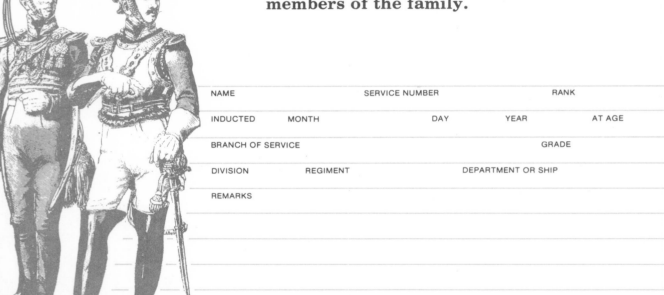

NAME		SERVICE NUMBER			RANK	
INDUCTED	MONTH		DAY	YEAR		AT AGE
BRANCH OF SERVICE				GRADE		
DIVISION		REGIMENT		DEPARTMENT OR SHIP		
REMARKS						

NAME		SERVICE NUMBER			RANK	
INDUCTED	MONTH		DAY	YEAR	AT AGE	
BRANCH OF SERVICE			GRADE			
DIVISION		REGIMENT		DEPARTMENT OR SHIP		DATES
REMARKS						

SERVICE NUMBER   RANK

        MONTH   DAY   YEAR   AT AGE

RVICE   GRADE

        REGIMENT   DEPARTMENT OR SHIP   DATES

SERVICE NUMBER   RANK

        MONTH   DAY   YEAR   AT AGE

ERVICE   GRADE

        REGIMENT   DEPARTMENT OR SHIP   DATES

            TRANSFERRED

NAME _____ SERVICE NUMBER _____ RANK _____

INDUCTED _____ MONTH _____ DAY _____ YEAR _____ AT AGE _____

BRANCH OF SERVICE _____ GRADE _____

DIVISION _____ REGIMENT _____ DEPARTMENT OR SHIP _____ DATES _____

REMARKS _____ TRANSFERRED _____

_____

_____

_____

_____

_____

_____

_____

NAME _____ SERVICE NUMBER _____ RANK _____

INDUCTED _____ MONTH _____ DAY _____ YEAR _____ AT AGE _____

BRANCH OF SERVICE _____ GRADE _____

DIVISION _____ REGIMENT _____ DEPARTMENT OR SHIP _____ DATES _____

REMARKS _____

_____

_____

_____

_____

_____

_____

_____

_____

_____

SERVICE NUMBER   RANK

MONTH   DAY   YEAR   AT AGE

ERVICE   GRADE

REGIMENT   DEPARTMENT OR SHIP   DATES

TRANSFERRED

SERVICE NUMBER   RANK

MONTH   DAY   YEAR   AT AGE

ERVICE   GRADE

REGIMENT   DEPARTMENT OR SHIP

DATES

Our Best Friends

A family register should also include close friends who, although not blood relations, are usually a part of the family life. Since a good friend is like a brother or sister—someone in whom we confide and with whom we share experiences—this book would be incomplete without a record of each one. So write down their names, addresses, when you knew them, and what it was that made the friends so special. Remember, too, that friends may be able to provide vital information about family members for you or future generations.

The Pets in Our Lives

For a child growing up, or even for an adult, a pet is like a special friend—a member of the family. Whether a cat, dog, horse, fish, turtle, monkey, or some more exotic creature, animals claim a daily part of a family's attention. In addition to recording vital statistics, therefore, try to create a portrait of each pet with a description of how it was acquired, its temperament, best tricks, favorite foods, and how you or the family cared for it.

_____

_____

_____

_____

_____

_____

_____

_____

_____

_____

_____

_____

_____

_____

_____

_____

_____

_____

_____

Automobiles

Our Mechanical Companions

Nothing has changed the character of modern living as radically as the automobile. Not only can we do errands, get to work or to school more quickly, but we can also travel long distances to visit friends and relations. In this way, the automobile plays an important role in almost every family's life. Moreover, each car owned by you or your family may help to recall special events or circumstances in the family story.

Special Things

Your special things reveal a great deal about your own personality. They may be sports, vacation spots, songs, recipes, and games. Or they may be objects like books, records, toys and paintings. In each case, a listing of these things forms a kind of brief character study, a written portrait of yourselves or your relatives.

Our Prized Family Possessions

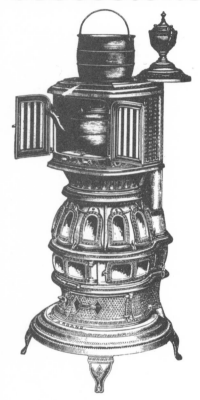

The objects passed down from generation to generation are as much a part of the family record as are names, dates, and events. Whether furniture, jewelry, art, a library, or a stamp collection, such things help make the past visible to the present. To read a book owned by your parents, or wear a necklace worn by your great-grandmother, or sit in the same chair in which your grandfather sat, is to become a living participant in your family's ongoing history. Try, therefore, to inventory the heirlooms, noting their original owners and how they came into your possession. Do the same for any collections formed by your ancestors that are still intact. And don't forget to include precious objects newly purchased or collections now being started, for these will be the heirlooms of tomorrow.

Our Prized Family Possessions

CONTINUED

Sports We Enjoy

Almost every family has someone who closely follows events in the sports world. You or a member of the family, however, may actually be a participant, either as a hobby or as a career. Who in your family, for example, plays or played tennis or football? With neighborhood friends, for a school team, or with a professional organization? Did you or a relative ever win an award? After listing the appropriate names, sports, and achievements, add any personal reminiscences about the people involved, or about a particularly exciting game that you remember playing in or attending.

Sports We Enjoy

CONTINUED

Our Family's Hobbies

What people do in their spare time, no matter how common or unusual, is often the most fascinating part of their personal histories. Have you a relative who makes pottery, breeds dogs, takes photographs, flies kites, does carpentry, collects butterflies, or sews? What hobbies do you pursue? Use this space to record the names and pastimes, how each person began, and what they accomplished. Are there any hobbies in which the entire family participates? Perhaps, too, you can recall a prize-winning achievement or have some treasured object that a relative made.

Our Family's Hobbies

CONTINUED

Memorable Vacations

For most of us, vacations are a wonderful break from everyday routine. We can relax and get away from it all without the pressures of school, work, or domestic responsibilities. Do you go on holidays by yourselves or does the whole family take off for the seashore, the ski slopes, or a cross-country journey? Some vacations no doubt made for memorable occasions. Describe them below—where you went, when, with whom—so that the family can relive these vacations and you can keep a precious record for later years.

Memorable Vacations

(CONTINUED)

Family Gatherings

Since many families do not reside in the same town, the family reunion is a joyful opportunity to see loved ones and renew cherished relationships. The reunions you describe here may have taken place by tradition at a particular time of the year, or the family may just have gotten together to celebrate holidays, special birthdays, or anniversaries. And whatever the occasion, use future meetings to gather information about the family's history. Don't forget to enter those reunions attended by the entire family, or a few of you.

Family Gatherings

CONTINUED

Cherished Traditions

*R*eunions are of course part of a family's traditions. But there are also customs in each family that live on, even when the members are separated, and help to give the family its own special character. It may be a special style of cooking handed down through the generations, or a unique way of commemorating birthdays. Is there a favorite repertory of stories invariably told to each generation of children? Whatever the traditions, enrich the picture of your family's heritage by entering them on these pages.

The Most Outstanding Events In Our Family's History

*T*here may be unusual events or special achievements in your family that cannot be easily categorized. Was anyone in the family, for instance, ever honored for outstanding service to their country or city? Did anyone make a technological invention or advance scientific knowledge? Perhaps a family member knew or met a famous personality, witnessed a history-making speech, or published a book. Use the space below to record these things.

The Most Outstanding Events In Our Family's History

CONTINUED

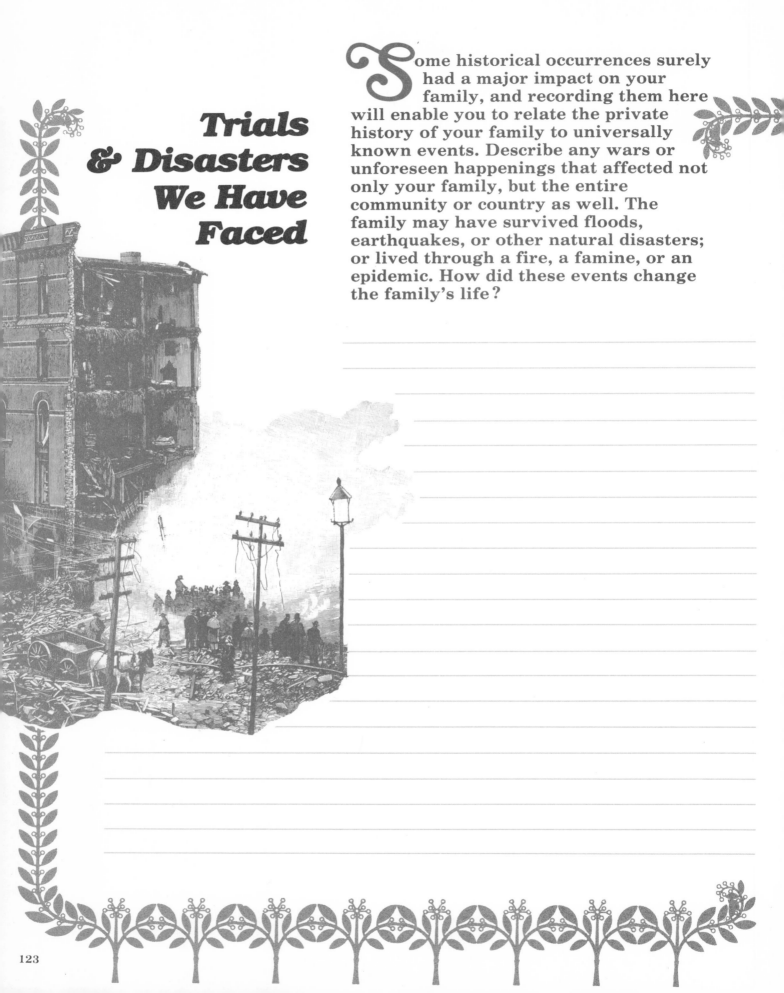

Trials & Disasters We Have Faced

Some historical occurrences surely had a major impact on your family, and recording them here will enable you to relate the private history of your family to universally known events. Describe any wars or unforeseen happenings that affected not only your family, but the entire community or country as well. The family may have survived floods, earthquakes, or other natural disasters; or lived through a fire, a famine, or an epidemic. How did these events change the family's life?

124

The Oral History of Our Family

Every family has stories that have been told from generation to generation. Such tales may involve heroic deeds, great achievements, fortunate escapes from disaster or political repression. Or they may recount personal anecdotes about how people met and married, where they traveled, and whom they knew. In all likelihood, these stories have never been written down. By doing so here you can preserve them for the future.

The Oral History of Our Family
CONTINUED

Our Family's Medical History

*I*llnesses are a sad but unavoidable feature of life. List here the names of those who were sick. Because some illnesses are hereditary, you may be recording vital information for future generations. In the remaining space, add your personal recollections and, if necessary, an account of how each illness altered the family's life.

_____
_____
_____
_____
_____
_____
_____
_____
_____
_____
_____
_____
_____
_____
_____
_____
_____
_____
_____
_____
_____
_____
_____
_____
_____
_____
_____

Our Vital Statistics

As we grow older, many things about us change. In this section you can record your present physical traits, clothes sizes, color preferences, and so on. The statistics will provide a handy guide for today, as well as give future generations a better idea of you. Along with the pictures in the photo section, you can look back, years from now, and see exactly what you and the family were like in 19 ____ .

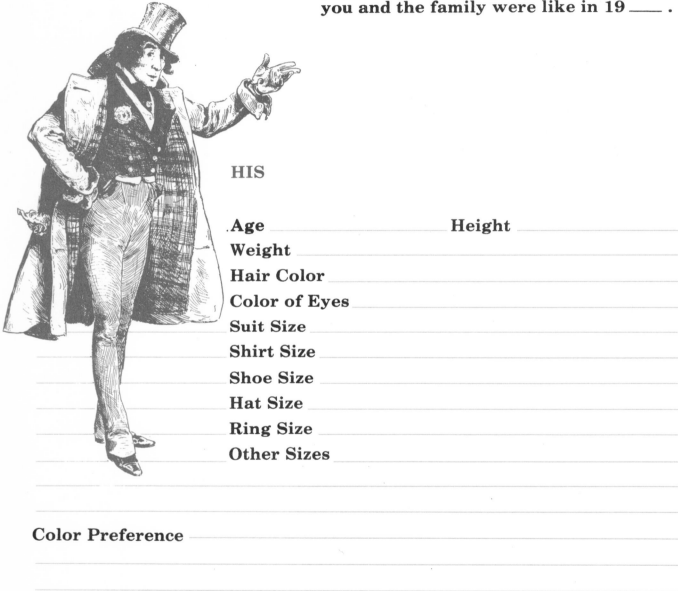

HIS

Age _____   Height _____

Weight _____

Hair Color _____

Color of Eyes _____

Suit Size _____

Shirt Size _____

Shoe Size _____

Hat Size _____

Ring Size _____

Other Sizes _____

_____

Color Preference _____

_____

Perfume & Toiletries Preference _____

_____

Height

olor

f Eyes

Size

Size

ze

ze

Sizes

Preference

ies Preference

CHILDREN	Age	Height	Weight	Hair Color

FAMILY

Our Vital Statistics

CONTINUED

r es	Suit Size / Dress Size	Blouse Size / Shirt Size	Shoe Size	Hat Size	Ring Size

Photographs

Pictures do their own story telling and in years to come a lot can be learned from this kind of record. You and future generations will be able to look back and see a member of the family in his or her own time and place. (You may also want to include favorite clippings, mementos, or documents.)

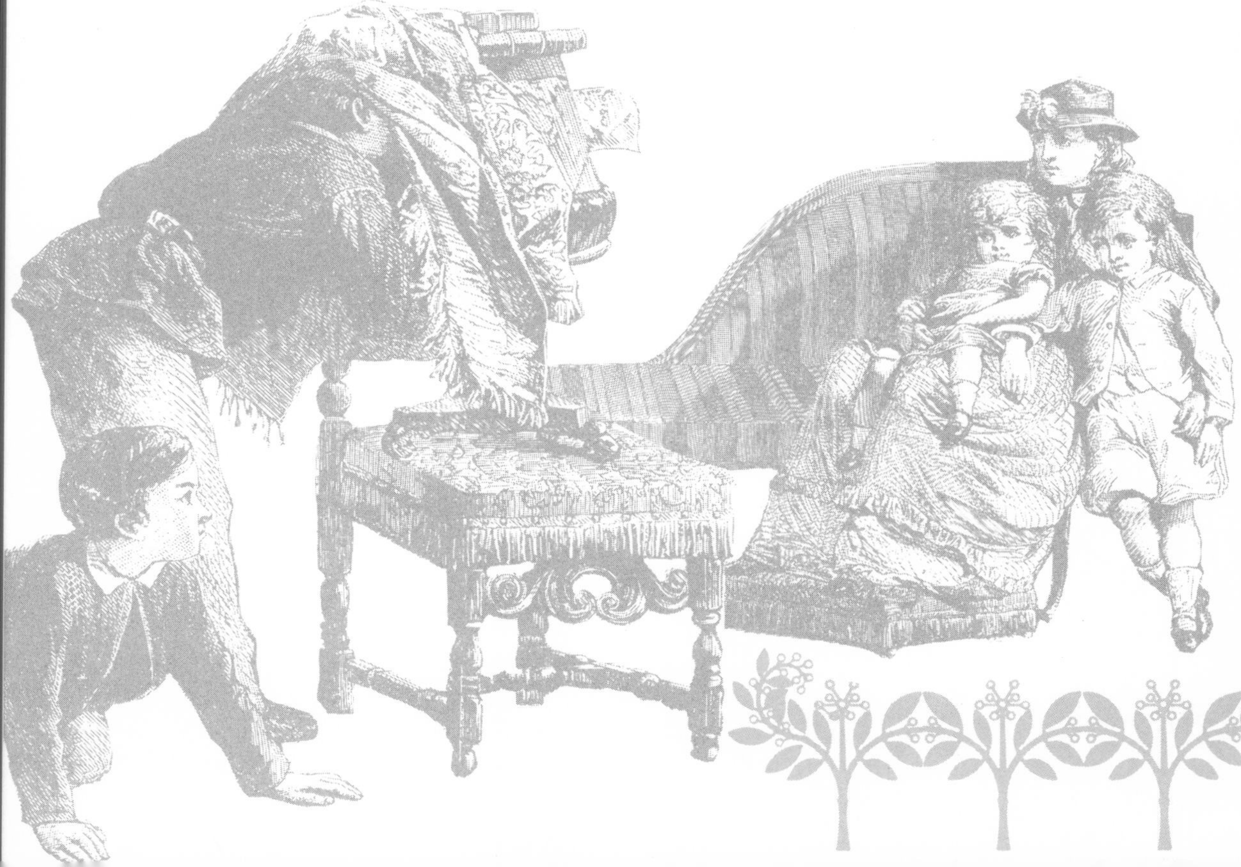

Photographs

CONTINUED

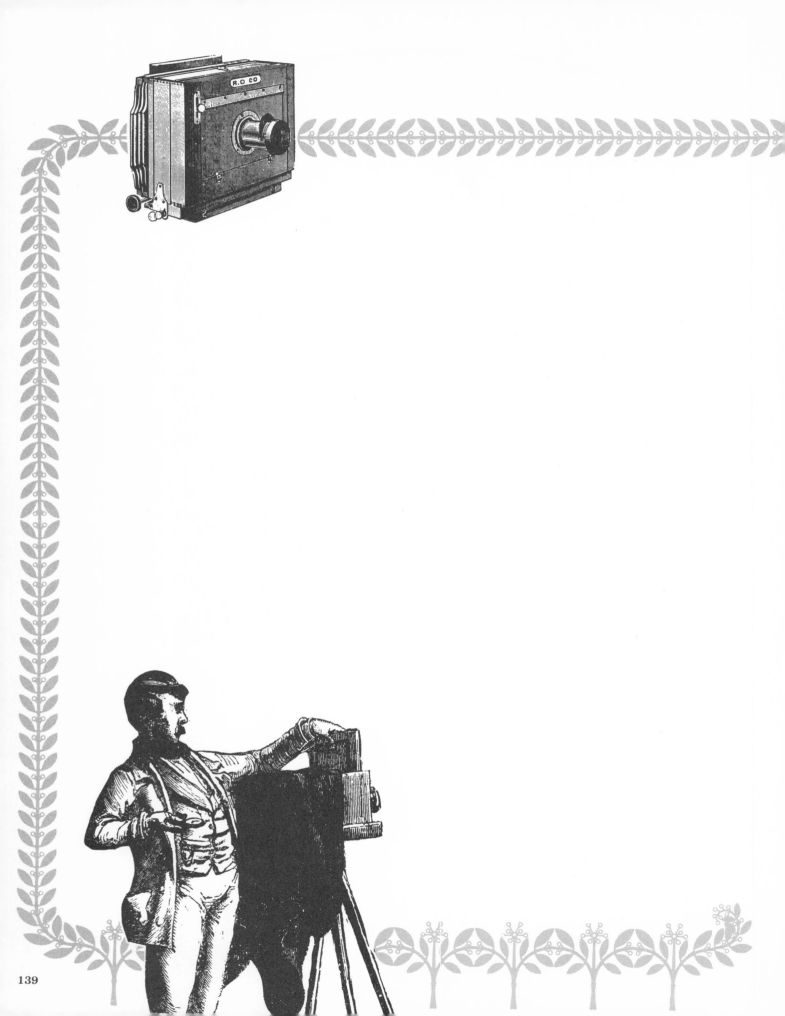

Photographs

CONTINUED

Genealogy Research

Genealogy research can be an enjoyable and rewarding experience if you approach it with curiosity and determination. Remember that you are carrying out this search to illuminate your own special history, so whatever you find will disclose a good deal about your heritage. Above all, don't get discouraged. Tracing ancestors can take you so far into the past and to such distant places that the task may sometimes seem hopeless. But, as experienced genealogists know, perseverance will win out. Moreover, your pursuit of history will open up worlds of new people, new places, and friendly organizations.

The procedure outlined here will start you on the right road. Where that road leads, how it branches off, will be determined by the unique make-up of your ancestral group. Because no one's heritage is like anyone else's, the possibilities are almost infinite. So after following the general suggestions, begin your own detective work, tracking down each clue as it comes in, writing to those agencies and using those reference books that are relevant to your particular quest. Once again, the task is less formidable than it seems. Genealogy is frequently a well-marked, step-by-step process, with one set of facts clearly pointing the way to the next. Each ancestor or each generation is bound to have some identifying feature—an occupation or a residence, for example—that

will tell you where to turn for information. It is as if your forebears were stretching their hands across time to guide you in your search.

Begin this search with the people around you. Interviewing relatives and family friends can uncover a wealth of names and statistics. Ask the family for the full names and dates of all the members they can recall. Don't be surprised if you suddenly learn of relatives you didn't know existed. People often forget about those who died a long time ago or who lived in another country and your questions will stimulate reluctant memories. Also ask relatives for any personal recollections about your ancestors. This is the only way to bring together the oral tradition of the family, which you now can preserve in written form.

Then start hunting—and encourage others to hunt—in attics, basements, and storerooms for family records. These records may take the form of documents, old letters, Bibles, photo albums, portraits, diaries, or even engraved jewelry and other heirlooms. Whatever you discover will no doubt supply additional names and dates, as well as a picture of the individuals. Even your grandmother's wedding dress or your grandfather's service medals are useful finds, for they reveal the kind of world in which these people lived and what they accomplished.

The telephone directory often turns out to be the genealogist's best reference tool. Local libraries usually keep old directories. Look for your surname in the ones that cover the period during which your family lived in the town. You may already know some of the names and the telephone book will tell you exactly where each person resided and, if you check from year to year, for how long. Don't forget to consider spelling changes in the family name. In addition, study the listings for your surname in a current directory. Are there any people with whom you are not acquainted? If so, send them the names and dates of your parents and grandparents and ask if they might be related. (Of course, if your surname is too common, this is not a practical step.) When you do come upon new relations in this way, ask them to try and fill in the missing pieces.

For the genealogist, even stones speak—tombstones, that is. Once you find out where an ancestor died, pay a visit to the local cemetery. A gravestone inscription will furnish the precise years of birth and death and sometimes even the months and days—statistics that are invaluable for future research. And the epitaph may disclose the name of a spouse, describe how the family felt about the deceased, or cite some impressive accomplishment. If no gravestone can be found, stop by at the cemetery office and check the records—not only for your known ancestors, but for those who bore the same name.

The next step is to pore over the records of the town in which you live or where your relations resided. All governments preserve records and local administrations are no exception. Armed with the ancestor's names and, if possible, significant dates, you may be able to reconstruct large parts of their lives with the information obtained from certificates of birth, marriage, divorce, or death; or from probated wills, tax and property assessments, and business incorporations or sales.

Schools are also inveterate record-keepers. Every public school, college, and university keeps a detailed account of its students. If you know where and approximately when someone was educated, ask the school authorities to check through the files for your relative's name. They just might hand you a marvelously complete report of grades, activities, and achievements!

Religious foundations, too, can be important sources of material. Most churches and synagogues maintain records of their congregations, or at least of the ceremonies that took place within their walls. And a certificate of baptism or confirmation, a copy of a wedding license or an entry for a funeral will supply essential names and dates. If you do not know to which congregation an ancestor belonged, visit or write to all the places of worship in the neighborhood where he or she resided.

The public library of every town or city is a storehouse of genealogical data. Not only does it house a good stock of reference books on the subject of genealogy research, but it probably has bound lists of births, marriages, and deaths, as well as copies of deeds and other civic documents—often dating back a century or more. Libraries also furnish old newspapers, usually preserved on microfilm. Take the date on which someone died and read the appropriate obituary columns for a mention of age, survivors, achievements, and the location of the funeral service.

Many towns, cities, states, counties, or provinces have local historical or genealogical associations that will be happy to offer assistance. Through them, moreover, you can meet other researchers with whom to exchange stories and share helpful hints.

Now you must move on to the national archives of your country— the repositories for all the vital statistics collected by census bureaus, immigration departments, and the armed forces. Census reports give you the age, occupation, place of birth, and exact residence of a relative during a particular year, in addition to the number and identity of the other family members living under the same roof. Immigration records contain the name of the ship on which someone

traveled, when it arrived, its port of entry, and the date of the immigrant's naturalization. A relative who worked for the government will also have a civil service record filed in the national archives. And remember that much of the information you seek can be solicited by letter.

It is at this point that each person's path of research branches out into innumerably diverse trails. The names and addresses of the national archives for the major English-speaking countries of the world appear at the end of this section. If they do not have the required data, they may advise you where to turn; or you may consult the reference books available in your library. By this time you will have accumulated enough details about your family's history to be able to exclude some avenues of research and focus sharply on others.

If you want to trace ancestors back to a foreign country, there are three basic lines of pursuit. First, many of the books in your library provide nation-by-nation lists of the names and addresses of people and agencies throughout the world who assist genealogists in hunting down foreign-born relatives. Second, write to the consulate of the country from which your family came—the address will be in the telephone directory or can be obtained from your own government. Consulates frequently put you in touch with the proper agency in their native lands. When requesting information from a foreign organization, be as specific as possible and try to cite all the spelling variations and name changes you have come across. Don't hesitate to write in English —your correspondent will find a translator.

Lastly, there is the Genealogical Society of the Church of Jesus Christ of Latter-day Saints (50 East North Temple Street, Salt Lake City, Utah 84150.) For the last eighty years, this remarkable group has been amassing an enormous collection of genealogical records from towns, cities, churches, and private groups all around the world. To date, they have almost a million 100-foot rolls of microfilm stored in deep mountain vaults, and the collection is increasing at the rate of 50,000 reels a year. Over seven million family groups and thirty million individuals are indexed in their archives. So no matter where you presently live or what country your ancestors came from, a letter to the Genealogical Society is an important step in your research.

Good luck!

National Archives

UNITED STATES
National Archives and Records Service
General Services Administration
Washington, D.C. 20408

CANADA
Public Archives of Canada
395 rue Wellington
Ottawa, Ontario K1A ON3

ENGLAND
Public Record Office
Chancery Lane
London WC2A 1LR, England

IRELAND
National Archives
Kildare Street
Dublin 2, Ireland

NORTHERN IRELAND
The Public Record Office
66 Balmoral Avenue
Belfast BJ9 6NY, Northern Ireland

SCOTLAND
Scottish Record Office
P.O. Box 36
H.M. General Register House
Edinburgh EH1 3YT, Scotland

WALES
National Library of Wales
Aberystwyth, Dyfed
S423 3BU, Wales

AUSTRALIA
National Archives
71 Leichhardt St., Kingston
Australian Capital Territory
2604 Australia

NEW ZEALAND
National Archives
Borthswick House
85 The Terrace
Wellington 1, New Zealand

SOUTH AFRICA
Central Archives Depot
Union Buildings
Private Bag X236
Pretoria, Rep. of South Africa, 0001

RHODESIA
National Archives of Rhodesia
Gun Hill, Borrowdale Road
Private Bag 7729
Causeway, Salisbury, Rhodesia

Name _____ **Relationship** _____

Street Address _____

City _____ **State** _____

Zip _____ **Telephone:** **Area** (   ) _____

Birth or Memorial Date _____ **Astrological Sign** _____

Name _____ **Relationship** _____

Street Address _____

City _____ **State** _____

Zip _____ **Telephone:** **Area** (   ) _____

Birth or Memorial Date _____ **Astrological Sign** _____

Name _____ **Relationship** _____

Street Address _____

City _____ **State** _____

Zip _____ **Telephone:** **Area** (   ) _____

Birth or Memorial Date _____ **Astrological Sign** _____

Name _____ **Relationship** _____

Street Address _____

City _____ **State** _____

Zip _____ **Telephone:** **Area** (   ) _____

Birth or Memorial Date _____ **Astrological Sign** _____

Addresses

Relationship _____

Address _____

State _____

Telephone: Area (_____) _____

Memorial Date _____   Astrological Sign _____

Relationship _____

Address _____

State _____

Telephone: Area (_____) _____

Memorial Date _____   Astrological Sign _____

Relationship _____

Address _____

State _____

Telephone: Area (_____) _____

Memorial Date _____   Astrological Sign _____

Relationship _____

Address _____

State _____

Telephone: Area (_____) _____

Memorial Date _____   Astrological Sign _____

Name _____ **Relationship** _____

Street Address _____

City _____ **State** _____

Zip _____ **Telephone: Area (** _____ **)** _____

Birth or Memorial Date _____ **Astrological Sign** _____

Name _____ **Relationship** _____

Street Address _____

City _____ **State** _____

Zip _____ **Telephone: Area (** _____ **)** _____

Birth or Memorial Date _____ **Astrological Sign** _____

Name _____ **Relationship** _____

Street Address _____

City _____ **State** _____

Zip _____ **Telephone: Area (** _____ **)** _____

Birth or Memorial Date _____ **Astrological Sign** _____

Name _____ **Relationship** _____

Street Address _____

City _____ **State** _____

Zip _____ **Telephone: Area (** _____ **)** _____

Birth or Memorial Date _____ **Astrological Sign** _____

Addresses

Relationship _____

Address _____

State _____

Telephone: Area (   ) _____

Memorial Date _____   Astrological Sign _____

Relationship _____

Address _____

State _____

Telephone: Area (   ) _____

Memorial Date _____   Astrological Sign _____

Relationship _____

Address _____

State _____

Telephone: Area (   ) _____

Memorial Date _____   Astrological Sign _____

Relationship _____

Address _____

State _____

Telephone: Area (   ) _____

Memorial Date _____   Astrological Sign _____

Autographs

Autographs

(CONTINUED)